RAILS IN THE WORTH VALLEY

65p

RAILS IN THE
WORTH VALLEY

by

PETER WILLIAMS

Dalesman Books
1973

THE DALESMAN PUBLISHING COMPANY LTD.,
Clapham (via Lancaster) Yorkshire.

First published 1973
© Peter Williams, 1973

ISBN: O 85206 179 X

Printed and bound in Great Britain by
FRETWELL & BRIAN LTD.
Silsden, Nr. Keighley, Yorkshire.

Contents

The cover illustration of Mytholmes viaduct is by Robin Lush.

Introduction

KEIGHLEY is a town of contrasts. It lies on the north-west edge of the textile complex of West Yorkshire where the grimy tentacles of industrial conurbation claw at the Pennine slopes as if reluctant to let go.

To the south-east of Keighley stretch mile after weary mile of millscape as town follows town, often with nothing more than a signpost to denote the transition from one to the next. All around are the monuments to an industrial society, the like of which will never be seen again; the stern factory blocks, many now silent or at best converted, with their sentinel chimneys standing dominant over rows of workers' dwellings. Here and there the drabness is relieved by a flowery garden display, a brightly painted door or a white cartwheel standing against the wall, but there is little other respite as one penetrates the teeming core of England's largest county.

Yet strike to the north-east of Keighley and within minutes the weight and gloom of the work-a-day world can be shrugged off as the eye roams freely over clear stretches of open moorland. While not actively encouraging plant or animal life, the region does support swishing grasses and scrubby heather, and a peculiar race of sheep who nervously resent the intrusion of man until it comes to using his roads on which to lie and ruminate. For the rambler who likes to traverse the rolling moors by footpath there are endless opportunities for relaxation, while easy access to the Pennine Way challenges the more experienced fell walker. Mill and moor could be a world apart.

Even the name of Keighley presents a contrast between the way it looks and the way it sounds; the "gh" is pronounced as "th". The town had its origins in the time of the industrial revolution and it is now a thriving manufacturing community. It boasts a handsome Town Hall, recently de-grimed, overlooking well-kept gardens with a nearby traffic-free pedestrian shopping precinct in the best style of the seventies. Retailing methods of a century ago are reflected in a fine parade of shops in the main street where a glazed wrought iron awning is provided to enable the shopper to stroll along the broad pavement under cover.

The visitor to Keighley, intrigued by this most convenient relic of yesteryear, may be tempted to take advantage of the protection it offers and embark on a window-shopping excursion down the gentle incline of the street. The sheltering presence of the awning and its elaborate ironwork may so lull him back through the years that he would attribute the distant train whistle and the plume of steam drifting over the rooftops to his wandering imagination. When he is jolted back from his reverie he will be surprised to find that these sounds and sights are still with him and, since it is a strange man who can ignore the lure of the steam train, thoughts of further window-shopping will evaporate as quickly as the vapour itself.

For it is at Keighley station, where the main line connects with the Worth Valley Branch, that steam and diesel rub shoulders. Every weekend throughout the year, and on many mid-week occasions, the past is brought to life here as steam locomotives hiss and huff along the platform and the smell of warm oil and coal smoke recall the greatest transport revolution this country has known. In this tiny corner of Yorkshire a complete railway has been re-created by the hands of men who do it for the love of it—men whose only reward for hours of work is seeing a job well done, men who would never have hoped that the venture would be half the succes it has turned out to be. This is the Keighley and Worth Valley Railway.

The Worth Valley branch was constructed and opened over one hundred years ago and operated by the Midland Railway; at the grouping in 1923 it came into the L.M.S. network, being taken over by British Railways at nationalisation in 1948. Steam was used exclusively on the line until 1960 when diesel railcars were brought into the valley, but the changing pattern of public transport brought about the withdrawal of even that facility and by mid-1962 the branch had closed completely. The Preservation Society was formed and restoration began in the mid-sixties; from that time the enterprise went from strength to strength and the re-opening special train was run in June 1968 amid great rejoicing. Work on the 5-mile track proceeded apace and the stations at Keighley, Ingrow, Damems, Oakworth,

Haworth and Oxenhope were cleaned up and brought back into use; previously discarded locomotives and rolling stock were purchased and brought to the line and work started on the gigantic task of their restoration. Services were improved, film contracts followed, more engines and carriages appeared and the public support which resulted soon stretched the resources of the railway to capacity. A passing loop was therefore constructed near Damems to enable two trains to be run simultaneously in opposite directions, and the railway could breathe again. Protection of the vast locomotive stud from the elements became a pressing problem and so covered accommodation was provided at Oxenhope; locomotives lovingly restored are thus kept clean and dry, secure from the ravages of weather and the hands of vandals, in sheds which must be the envy of the steam fraternity.

The local residents may have sceptical views of the railway. Indeed, in the year 1840 a most famous daughter of the valley, Charlotte Bronte, wrote: "A distant relative of mine . . . has set off to seek his fortune in the wild, wandring, adventurous, romantic, knight-errant-like capacity of clerk on the Leeds and Manchester Railroad." Tongue in cheek, maybe, but in the Worth Valley of today the sceptics are falling silent.

Keighley

On Keighley station the Keighley & Worth Valley Railway (KWVR) extends the usual courtesy of permitting other preserved railways to advertise in a colourful display.

Entering the station from street level, one descends a covered way whose walls are tiled in the best traditions of other public places.

A change of decor is immediately apparent on the approach to the KWVR platform.

While other platforms at Keighley station are owned and used by British Railways, the KWVR platform is exclusive.

Countless hours of renovation have gone into smartening up the premises to their present state.

The detail here will be of interest to modellers. The rail-built buffer stop terminates the KWVR line; on its left is a small sales office operated by the Vintage Carriages Trust.

Cast iron brackets, decorative mouldings . . .

. . . and fluted pillars are all original and form attractive features of the platform awning.

One of the privileges of the engine driver is to have a reserved seat on the platform for relaxation between trips.

...anding by the booking office is
...venerable platform ticket mach-
...e—it is fully operative and old
...nnies required to feed it may be
...btained at the ticket office. Also
...iginal is the departure indicator.

They just don't build platforms and fittings like this any more. It is interesting to note that all the engines are orientated with their smokeboxes towards Oxenhope and their bunkers towards Keighley; there are no turning facilities on the line and therefore all trains arrive at Keighley being hauled by a locomotive running in reverse. As there is no run-round loop in the station itself, all trains have to be moved back to the station approach where this operation can take place. With the engine in its conventional position, the carriages are then reversed into the platform, as shown here, to await the next departure.

The paved platform with its trim floral tubs is the scene of excitement and haste as departure time draws near.

But it is at the head of the train where the interest for most visitors to the line lies. Here will be found a living, breathing reincarnation of the glory that was steam.

A visit to the line on any weekend will find one of a dozen different locomotives doing the only job a locomotive looks right doing—standing in a crinoline of steam before easing into the graceful powerful motion that is such a delight to the eye.

Let it not be forgotten that were it not for the voluntary work of a thousand pairs of hands (to say nothing of the support of an eager public), these proud giants of the past might have disappeared altogether, or at best be rotting hulks in the breaker's yard.

The demand for water could surely never have been as great as now with a stable of ever-thirsty engines to support.

With the coming of the diesel the water tower at Keighley must have been regarded as having reached the end of its days. It was a happy accident that allowed it to survive for a new, undreamed of, lease of life.

It is the fashion nowadays to criticise the pollutive thoughtlessness of our industrial forbears — but surely there are exceptions to every rule.

Just beyond the station limits at Keighley stands a derelict signal box; from its elevated operating floor this sequence of photographs was taken. As the exhaust blast echoes round the factory blocks, the train approaches the points at the end of the run-round loop.

A close-up of the engine as it clatters up the 1 in 60 gradient.

The sight and sound of the exhaust become synchronised as the train approaches.

Working hard, the engine heads the train round the sharp curves outside Keighley.

It gathers speed on the approach to a road overbridge.

Another view of No. 41241 on the sharp curve
just outside Keighley station.

Ingrow

Ingrow station is overlooked by a stern church tower.

In the yard there stands the goods crane, a fine example of this type of railway hardware. The side frames and balance weights flow in graceful curves, and recall an age when it was not considered an extravagance to produce a piece of equipment which combined visual appeal with mechanical efficiency.

The point mechanism at Ingrow is rarely used as most traffic goes straight through, but the goods siding was used as temporary accommodation for a new addition to the motive power fleet. This is Mr. Riddles' design for the BR Standard Class 4; numbered 75078, it is to be fully restored and put into use on the line by the efforts of a separate group.

Ingrow tunnel takes the line under the main Keighley to Halifax road . . . .

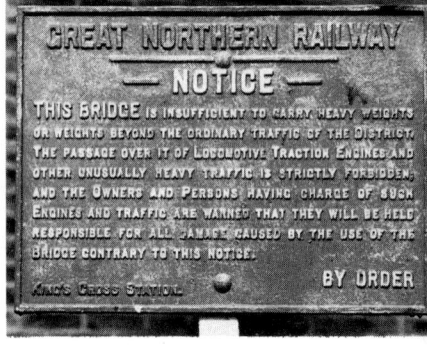

. . . . a road which later crosses the disused trackbed of the old Great Northern line from Keighley to Queensbury. At the bridge stand these two cast-iron notices which no doubt catch the eye of many a passing motorist.

Damems

At Damems station there is abundant evidence that, even if your only talent is a green thumb, there is a job for you on your local preserved railway.

The station is really in the country and the platform is only the length of one carriage; it is a cosy halt in a charming setting.

Features which give Damems station an atmosphere of its own include the sheltering trees . . . .

33

. . . . the well-tended flower beds, and the white-painted fence-work.

The house and the crossing keeper's hut are the only buildings
at the station itself. Just beyond the level-crossing gate lies
the passing loop which permits up and down trains to cross.

Oakworth

Oakworth station, of "Railway Children" fame, could be said to be the best preserved on the line.

Architecturally the station building is pure Midland and it completely blends with its surroundings; the Ladies Room on the left appears to be a later extension.

The platform seats have cast ironwork obviously intended for branch lines.

The station boasts many fine gas lamps, both wall-mounted and free-standing. The cold yellow light from hissing gas mantles is recalled . .

. . . in vintage posters carefully chosen to be in keeping with the period. Other advertisements, many in original enamel, adorn the station fence and bring a colourful breath of yesteryear to the platform.

Oakworth
Level Crossing

BEWARE OF TRAINS.

MIDLAND RAILWAY.

7 VICT. CAP. 18 SEC. 238 ENACTS "THAT IF ANY
PERSON SHALL BE OR TRAVEL OR PASS UPON FOOT
UPON THE MIDLAND RAILWAY WITHOUT THE
LICENSE AND CONSENT OF THE MIDLAND RAILWAY
COMPANY, EVERY PERSON SO OFFENDING SHALL
FORFEIT AND PAY ANY SUM NOT EXCEEDING TEN
POUNDS FOR EVERY SUCH OFFENCE."
NOTICE IS THEREFORE HEREBY GIVEN THAT ALL
PERSONS FOUND TRESPASSING UPON THIS RAILWAY
OR THE WORKS THEREOF WILL BE PROSECUTED.

JUNE 1906.   ALEXIS L. CHARLES.
                              SECRETARY.

The crossing sports original lamp fittings and signalling equipment. It is operated by an exposed lever frame which stands near some cast sign-boards.

Between Oakworth and Haworth lies Mytholmes tunnel; just to the south is a road overbridge which affords pleasant views of the rural setting of the line.

Haworth

Haworth station follows the Midland blueprint and the building contains a booking office, a light refreshment counter and a thriving sales area.

Haworth itself is the mecca of visiting enthusiasts whether they arrive by train from Keighley . . . .

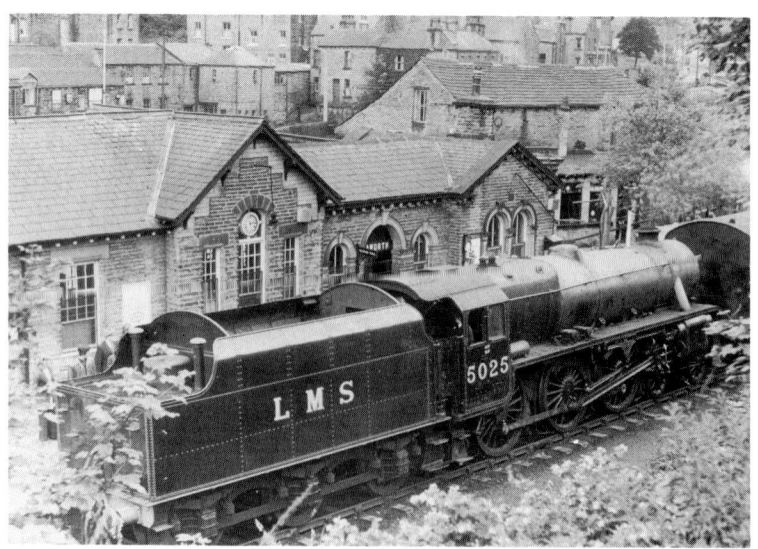

. . . . or Oxenhope.

The station stands aloof from the rest of Haworth where the hilly slopes have dictated the adoption of curious styles of house-building.

But to most onlookers a more stirring sight is the steam locomotive in all its whispy grandeur

45

The Haworth yard offers opportunities for the onlooker which never existed when steam ruled the rails. Row after row of carriages and engines are there to browse and stroll along at leisure. A closer inspection is imperative.

The oldest inhabitant stands by one of the gas lamps at the gate . . .

..... "Bellerophon" was built in 1874 and incorporates many unusual features for an industrial locomotive—for instance Mr. Gooch's outside valve gear is used to drive piston valves. The attractive curve from smokebox to cylinders is typical of locomotive design of a century ago; the 4-wheeled coach in film make-up looks well behind the engine.

By the other gas lamp can be seen the clerestory roof of another venerable acquisition. This carriage was built in six-wheeled form for the Locomotive Superintendent of the North Eastern Railway in 1871; later extended and mounted on bogies, it is now the oldest standard gauge passenger coach still running.

The Pullman cars at Haworth recall an age of elegance with their oval windows, pebbled glass, leaded lights and brass fittings. "Zena," built in 1928, was the first of the KWVR Pullmans. The second Pullman was delivered as Car No. 84, but the new owner subsequently renamed it after his wife. Standing in the foreground are the tender wheels from Mr. Bulleid's pacific locomotive, to be seen later.

No. 3924 represents Mr. Fowler's 1911 design for the Midland Railway 0-6-0 goods locomotive, although the tender now fitted is of a later design. The 4F was rescued from the scrapyard in 1968 and is now fully restored and running again in black LMS livery.

Industrial locomotives are by far the most numerous among the ranks of the preserved as many of them continued in service long after the withdrawal of BR steam. One suspects there is some affection in the use of their nickname at Haworth—"The Uglies"—for there is nothing ugly about the front end of No. 62 compared with the square-block radiator of the diesel shunter.

No. 5025 is an example of Mr. Stanier's ubiquitous Class 5 which has seen much service on the KWVR of late. At the time of writing this engine is destined for the Aviemore-Boat of Garten project in Scotland.

Built in 1934 at the Vulcan Foundry, Lancashire, and overhauled by Hunslet in 1969, this carefully restored engine is now running in lined black LMS livery. The class is noted for its ability to cope with trains of all sorts and sizes.

Now sporting green Southern livery, this coach was built to a design by Mr. Bulleid.

The latest design of the company crest bears the words "Keighley and Worth Valley Light Railway."

Mr. Bulleid also designed No. 34092 "City of Wells." The striking monolithic appearance of the original West Country design could well have been ahead of its time when it was introduced in 1945, while the unique cast steel wheels had many advantages over the spoked type.

A line-up of locomotives at Haworth almost dwarfs the delightful 0-4-0 tank "Lord Mayor."

"Lord Mayor" has been restored to as near original condition as one can get with an 80-year old locomotive.

Privately-owned and on loan to the KWVR, this 15-ton sprite receives gentle treatment. A close inspection of it reveals many interesting features.

No. 72 was built in the U.S.A. and brought to England for use in the south, being allocated to Guildford in 1946. It was withdrawn from BR service in 1967 and came to Haworth shortly afterwards. The engine is quite distinctive in appearance—it is an extrovert which just has to have three of everything.

Sporting aluminium-painted smokebox and steampipes
(should they not be chromium-plated?), No. 72 with its
brown livery and chime whistle is very much part of the
Worth Valley scene.

This fine example of the BR Standard Class 4 tank engine has been lovingly restored at Haworth and, although it was designed by Mr. Riddles, the influence of Messrs. Fowler, Fairburn and Stanier can be seen.

After withdrawal from BR service the locomotive was used as a carriage heating boiler in Scotland for several years, but the care and attention that have gone into its restoration have recreated the appearance it must have had the day it emerged from Derby works in the early fifties.

Of Lancashire & Yorkshire ancestry, being built about the turn of the century, the 0-4-0 pug was one of the first arrivals at Haworth. It is in the care of the L&Y Saddletanks Group.

This 0-6-0 tank in unlined black was used on the Manchester Ship Canal Railway. At the outbreak of the Kaiser war the nameplates were removed in view of strong local feeling, but the original name has been restored since the engine arrived at Haworth in 1967.

A much later arrival is No. 48431, an example of the 8F class of Mr. Stanier. It would be easy to say that the weight of train likely to be hauled on the KWVR would be well within the capacity of this powerful freight locomotive, but the mounting public attendance at the railway could well put such a prophecy in question.

While all the pre-nationalisation groups are represented on the KWVR, the Great Western contingent is minimal. This brake, with grey paintwork and white lettering and hand-railing, is the vehicle which features in the "Brake Van Special" trips. These are out-of-seaon excursions run for Society members only when a smaller or lesser used locomotive is given an airing with the nominal load of one vanful of assorted enthusiasts.

Contrasting styles of buffer design.

A medley. On the left, Mr. Johnson's 0-6-0 ex-Midland tank which, as No. 41708, ended its days with BR as the oldest locomotive then in service; behind, the BR 4MT; on the right, an "Ugly."

A black painted tank wagon is one of the few goods wagons on the railway.

The 500 h.p. diesel locomotive is indispensable for the shunting of rolling stock and dead engines and is frequently used on works trains.

A gift to the railway from I.C.I., this trim Andrew Barclay saddle tank is smartly turned out in its blue livery and neat lining; the maker's number was 2226.

Another Great Western representative is the No. 5775 of Mr. Collett. One of the very numerous 5700 class built at Swindon, this 0-6-0 pannier tank spent some time with London Transport before coming to Haworth in 1970.

This Peckett 0-4-0 saddle tank of 1941 was happily acquired by the railway for a nominal sum; it is to be named "Darwen" in recognition of the engine's previous home at the gas works there.

Designed by Mr. Riddles, this 0-6-0 saddle tank was built for the War Department in 1945 by Robert Stephenson & Hawthorn of Newcastle for the Longmoor Military Railway. A year later it went to the Manchester Collieries where it acquired its curious name and, after modification by Hunslet in 1963, came to Haworth in 1969.

For off-peak services the railway operates two diesel railcars. They were built in 1958 at Donauworth, West Germany, for service on BR and operated in Derbyshire and East Anglia until withdrawal. Since coming to Haworth in 1967 they have had their control gear modified so that they may be coupled together and run as a multiple unit.

An evocative view of the Haworth yard with its atmosphere of bustling activity, drifting smoke, clanging fire-irons and scraping shovels.

More Lancashire & York-shire hardware in the shape of the saddle tank No. 752. Now beauti-fully restored in black livery lined red and white (the colours of the roses) this is the tank version of a tender locomotive to be featured later.

That the restoration is no skin-deep job is evident from the pristine machinery visible beneath the frames. The L&Y crest has had to be hand-painted.

Another of the railway's workhorses is the 2-6-2T of Mr. Ivatt, No. 41241. It is smartly turned out in crimson lake livery with black edging and a straw line, and was privileged to head the festive train when the line reopened in 1968.

Much care and pride are evident in the appearance of No. 41241; here the lubricators are being topped up prior to the day's work.

With a last look at the Haworth yard . . . .

. . . . it is time to leave Haworth and travel the final mile to
Oxenhope. Long ago, a son of the village by the name of
Branwell Brontë left Haworth "to become a booking-clerk
at a small station called Sowerby Bridge."

Almost immediately after leaving Haworth the line settles into a steady 1 in 68 gradient which is maintained almost until Oxenhope is reached.

The route meanders up the valley alongside Bridgehouse Beck.

Oxenhope

Behind the platform at Oxenhope stands this ex-Midland Railway six-wheeler dating from 1886 and now under restoration by the Vintage Carriages Trust.

The station building follows the now-familiar style of architecture. In addition to the usual facilities, refreshment and souvenir sales are conducted in a converted carriage to the rear of the curved platform. The run-round loop starts in a newly-excavated run-on extension, alongside which a water tower awaits erection. Increased seating on the platform will be provided after the repainting of these acquisitions from the Mersey Docks & Harbour Board.

The rural setting of Oxenhope contrasts strongly with industrial Keighley at the other end of the line.

The provision of genuine platform accessories, whether actually used or not, shows the little touches of detail that add credibility to this re-creation of times past.

A privately owned Sheffield tram provides an interesting diversion in the yard.

The striking appearance of the ex-LNER observation coach never fails to excite attention even in these modern times; the effect when it first appeared on the Coronation trains in 1937 must have been most dramatic. Purchased and restored to showroom condition by the Gresley Society, it is unfortunately not suitable for use on KWVR trains at the moment.

This terraced property, late of the Metropolitan Railway, can now be found at Carriage Sidings, Oxenhope Station, Yorkshire.

Built at Doncaster for the Great Northern Railway in 1888, the original teak exterior of this coach has survived in a remarkable condition It has been preserved by the Vintage Carriages Trust.

The diagonal steps and curved handrail are typical features of this Midland representative of a type of carriage which was almost certainly used on the Worth Valley branch in the years preceding World War I.

This six-wheeler started its days as a personal carriage for Mr Raven in the North Eastern Railway period; it is one of three York-built V.I.P. coaches to have survived into KWVR hands. In later service with BR the open verandah made it an ideal vehicle for tunnel inspection; hence the floodlights mounted on the roof.

Another Vintage Carriage Trust acquisition, this four-wheeled tri-composite coach boasts one first, one second, two thirds and a baggage compartment. It was built in 1876 for the Manchester, Sheffield & Lincolnshire Railway.

Clearly the new shed at Oxenhope is intended for the storage of dead engines only. Doubtless, its clean paintwork and light and airy interior encourage the visitor to browse among the fascinating exhibits inside.

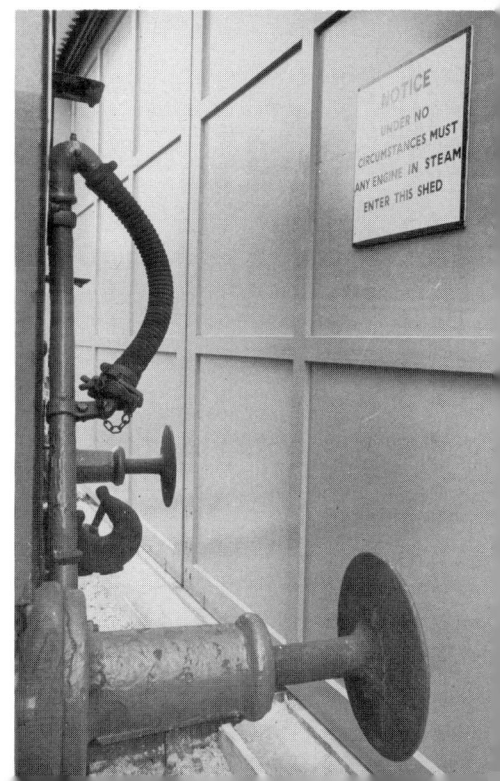

An advantage of having covered accommodation available is that it can be used for the storage of immobile locomotives from which parts have been removed for maintenance or replacement. These views show 45212, 2700 and 1708.

The shape of things to come was foretold in the high running plate of 2700, a "Crab" 2-6-0 built in 1926 at Horwich and at present on loan from BR.

The Rochdale group of the Society was responsible for the restoration of the L&Y tank No. 752 in a neighbourly exercise of inter-county co-operation.

The KWVR's own Black Five has the historical distinction of being the last steam locomotive in BR service to haul a scheduled passenger train.

The J72 tank was introduced by Mr. Worsdell in 1878, and this engine was one of the last to be produced by BR in 1951. It has been restored to apple green livery and named "Joem" after the owner's parents—Joseph and Emmiline.

The smaller shed at Oxenhope is a new structure added as an extension to the original stone goods shed. Viewed over the front end of the "Crab" is the smokebox of the Lancashire & Yorkshire 0-6-0 tender locomotive, No. 957.

Sir Nigel Gresley is represented by this example of his N2 class, an 0-6-2 tank locomotive of powerful proportions. The hefty condenser pipes are a distinctive feature of this design.

No. 957 was built in 1887, and came to Haworth in 1965. It has since been completely restored and now appears in NER-type apple green livery with black bands and white lining.

The Manning Wardle 0-6-0 industrial tank is another privately owned attraction at Oxenhope. Dating from 1891, the engine was used in the construction of the Manchester, Sheffield & Lincolnshire Railway. The engine, fitted with a weather-protective cab, remained in use until 1963. The cab was later removed when the original brass-trimmed spectacle plate was happily re-discovered, and "Sir Berkeley" now appears in its original condition.

Meanwhile, outside on the platform a train has arrived. No. 72 has run round its rake of carriages, replenished at the temporary water tower and in a few moments will be setting off on yet another journey to Keighley.

Peace once more descends on the platform at Oxenhope. On the departing train another party of visitors is carried back to the outside world; back to the kitchen stove, to the office desk, to the workbench. Just for a while they have been transported back in time into the railway age and have experienced the sights and sounds and smells of a generation ago, brought back to life by a band of enthusiasts who do it just for the love of it—because it is there; a band whose motives may sometimes be held to question now, but a band from whom future generations will inherit a living legacy.

For the future of the Keighley and Worth Valley Railway must be assured; it has got to be in the front rank of steam preservation centres with its attractive facilities and convenient location. The wide range of exhibits entrusted to it by other bodies is an indication of the confidence held in it—confidence born of past achievements and of bold plans for the future. It is the fire of enthusiasm that has brought steam back to the Worth Valley; let there long be fuel for the flame.